My Own John Lennon Poems from the Heart

Mary Elizabeth Down

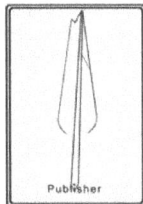

Publisher

MA PUBLISHER

Mary Elizabeth Down

Produced by MAPublisher for Penny Authors
Email: Pennyauthors@yahoo.co.uk
www.pennyauthors.org.uk

Published by MA Publishing (Penzance)
Email: mapublisher@yahoo.com
www.mapublisher.org.uk

Will be printed in the regions the books have been purchased: Australia | Canada | Europe | UK | USA

ISBN-13: 9781915958211

Cover designed by Mayar Akash
Cover photo taken by Mary Elizabeth Down
Typeset in Times Roman

Paper printed on is FSC Certified, lead free, acid free, buffered paper made from wood-based pulp. Our paper meets the ISO 9706 standard for permanent paper. As such, paper will last several hundred years when stored.

2

Dedication

This book of Poems from the Heart is dedicated to the memory of
Alan.

It is also dedicated to my family and to all my friends who have
supported me along the way

Acknowledgements

My heartfelt thanks to Mayar Akash for awakening my desire to publish my poems, the majority of which have languished on top of my bookcase in their cloth-covered exercise books patiently waiting for this moment - so thank you Mayar and all your 'penny authors' may you all succeed in your own quests.

I would also like to thank my children, Lucy Phaedra and Taro who have grown up along the said exercise books and read and admired them for what they are.

My thanks go to all my friends who have encouraged me on this journey to see my poems in print, my steadfast friend Sandra, my hairdresser Corinne, my friends Nikki, Chris and Annie and all the staff at Rhubarb and Mustard.

Thank you to every one of my friends who I have forgotten to mention.

Lastly, I would like to give thanks to Alan for his love and for travelling the world with me - but who sadly crossed the Rubicon too soon to be able to see this book in print

CONTENT

Introduction

I began this journey in a second-hand bookshop when I picked up a book of poetry which caught my eye, it was called Res's Writing, Poetry and pictures by Res J F Burman. I was fascinated by his poems and pictures. After reading it I went on line to find out more about Res and was invited to comment on his poetry which I did.

A couple of weeks later I received a phone call from M.A.Publishing and spoke to Mayar Akash who knew Res who unfortunately had died recently. After a long conversation with Mayar, I said I had always kept my own poems but had never got around to publishing them.

Mayar said he wanted to help me publish my poems - and so this poetry book is the result of that phonecall for which I shall always be grateful for.

I started writing poems from an early age, a collection of my observations on life and loves and reactions to the world in general; the war in Vietnam, for the suffering that victims and soldiers go through, for injustices in the world.

My poems are loosely arranged in chronological order from when I started putting my thoughts on paper to the present day.

It channels my life from teenage angst to leaving home, to love and marriage, to children, the love of motherhood and finding my way in the world, from falling in love again and again, finally finding the love of my life and my love of travel, from bereavement to acceptance finally to peace within oneself.

There will always be wars and, as I tell my children, there will always be someone worse off than yourself.

I hope you enjoy my poems as much as I did making this book. Happy reading.

My John Lennon

We were in Turkey
At a resort in Bodrum
A Turkish waiter said to Alan
Are you John Lennon?
No, sorry, I'm Alan
You look like John Lennon
I don't think he believed us

After that the Turks all called him John Lennon
Good morning John Lennon
How are you today John Lennon?
To me, he was a lot nicer than John Lennon
He was my man
Maybe I was his Yoko
I suppose he was always making jokes like John Lennon did

But I bet John Lennon didn't play the mouth organ
Like Alan did
And I bet John Lennon didn't dance
As well as Alan did
When we used to dance
With pleasure
Together

With pleasure
Together

The Dawn of Creation

When all the world was sleeping and patient
Our eyes were watching
A Creation
Black curtains of night enfolding us
Diamonds staring down at us
Meteors flashing through the sky
Joining heaven to earth
For us to see
A fantasy
Eyes wide glued to skies
Watching this paradise
Of colours blend
Sky turns to ebony
Clouds turn to castles
And spread across the sky
Like a beach of moving sand
On the surface of the moon
Moving sliding silently across the sky
For us to see the dawn
Approaching
The blanket of night lifts from the East
And mysterious shapes appear in the clouds
Suddenly the sky is filled
With light and dark
With blacks and greys and blues
And the clouds in the East turn to purple
Then to pink
A shade of Crimson velvet grows
And glows
Enfolds itself into the sky
Moving like fire burns
Gently as water turns
A sea aflame a Crimson torch
Magnificent in its glory
And from red it turns to burnished gold
Without a sound

Part Two of the Dawn of Creation

A secret of the universe
Alone
And it gently subsides
To let a ray appear from the midst
And from the sides a crown of golden rays appear
Heralding the wake of the Sun
Slowly gently the gold has turned to yellow
As the small cloud parts
As a curtain
To let a light appear
A white radiance of light
A tiny jewel
And with our eyes
We see the sight
Of the Sun
The mystery of the universe
The King of the sky
The Creation
The Word
No words to say
To wonder
At the beauty in the sky
And the seagulls cry

Things Are

A poet sits and writes his verse
Of nature's life and beauty
A painter studies silently
Scenes of people town and country
The music maker plays his tune
And recreates his memory lane
Of feelings scenes and faces
An artist is a poet and a poet is an artist
The musician gently blends the two
To put into his music
Who can understand the picture

cont.

When the artist draws his thoughts
Who can picture the story
The music maker sought
You can read my poems
And criticise or frown
But my poems are my story
And my story is my own
Pictures of what's in my mind
Memories and thoughts
Try to look through my eyes
Then look through yours as an afterthought

Until We Go To Heaven

My mother didn't see me the day that I was born
Only the next door neighbour saw
How I almost choked on the cord.
I lived in a book of fairy tales and dreams
When I was a child
And I woke up at fourteen years
And got drunk of Somerset cider
And then I ran away from home three times
Trying to be free
And I was introduced to Paki-black*
When I was 16
Speed and barbs and mandies arrived
And I loved everyone
Sometime later after that
I was shown some Opium
I finally walked away from home
And secretly had a baby
And lived with The Salvation Army from 1970
Whilst there I had some LSD
Which opened up my eyes
I started smoking dope again and
Blew up my mind
Soon I found a little flat and turned it into heaven
I shared with lots of others
But always felt unstable
But there was always something else   cont.

Missing in my home
Till I went out one special day and got attached to someone and then I fell
in love with him
And now he is my husband
Ti's not the story of my life
My story's just beginning
For who knows what the future holds
Until we get to heaven
I don't know where I'm going but I know
Where I have been
All my life I've been searching for all the things I need
Now I've found love and peace and happiness
And I've a home. I've a husband and a little girl
I'm no longer alone
We've many years ahead of us
The door of life's still open
For who knows what the future holds
Until we get to Heaven

* The resin compressed out of the cannabis plant has other names—Plain
old Hashish, Paki Black (meaning from Pakistan in particular),

Jan Finka

It was the first time I fell in love
And I fell in love with his smile first off
He told me his name was John Smith
The first time I met him cos he had a reputation

I told them at school about him
They said it sounded like Jan Finka
So I told him this the next time I met him
Especially when his mates called him Yan

He said "Will you still go out with me
If I was Jan Finka?" "Yes" I said
I am he said, and so we were one me and Jan
Four years of excitement and exhilaration

At our next meeting I had to go with him cont.

To see his probation officer and let him know
I was going to keep him on the right path,
On the straight and narrow - and so it began

I had to call him Roger when he phoned
My parents had heard the rumours
Not much escaped our village
Especially when he phoned the fire brigade

In the dead of night with the fire alarms blaring
And bright lights dazzling they arrived
In the morning he'd phone me up laughing
And sang "it's the fire brigade the fire brigade"

He was in and out of Borstal for stealing
Gave me a diamond necklace once
"How can I ever wear that?" I said
But it sparkled as I hid it in my top drawer

He scratched out our names
On Bristol suspension bridge
Then died in a fight with his mate
RIP JAN - my young man

Spring Flower

The flower opened up
And let the sun
Inside
Can you open up your heart
If I open mine
To you?

And when the sun went down
The flower closed
Slowly
Just as you
Shut your heart
To me
And wouldn't let me in

cont.

And in the spring
A bud grew
On the flower
As my love grows
For you
Open your heart up
Now

For soon that flower
Will die
And as it withers
The petals will fall
As my tears
Are falling now
For you

And I hope next spring
Another flower will open to the sun
And let me in
Although I know
It won't be yours

Philip Claxton

I saw him cycling out of the factory
In his hippie shirt with blonde hair flying
And blue eyes smiling
I was in love - again

He played a guitar to me beautifully
We walked the canals peacefully
And lay on the grace completely
In love

We hitched to places we hadn't seen
Explored beaches in a dream
In his Jethro Tull hippie hat
And his flowery shirts

He thought hippies would change the world

cont.

That love and peace would overcome
That protest marches would end
The war in Vietnam

He leant me records, Leonard Cohen
Songs from a room, The Doors L.A. Woman
The Byrds Fifth Dimension Roy Harper Flat Baroque
And Beserk and Family in a Dolls House

But life took me on a different road
I came to live in a different town
But he phoned me and played his guitar to me
And sang "You've got a friend in me"
I wonder where you are now
Philip Claxton my pretty hippie
With your blue eyes and pink cheeks
And your hippie hat

The Mother and Baby Home

Looking like a castle
With baby prams on the veranda
Welcomed by a Sally Army lady
I wanted to go home
But could not

A room full of pregnant girls
Staring at me, newcomer
They were always crying at night
I wanted to go home
But could not

All in the same boat
We made friends
Knowing eventually we would lose our bumps
And have our babies taken away from us

Babies once loved and hugged briefly
Were taken away from them
And girls once so young and free

cont.

Now sobbed and grieved

We held them while they cried
As the cars drove away with their babies inside
They had to go home acting fine
While all inside their hearts had died

I gave birth to my beautiful daughter
Then when the time came to part with her
And I had to give her up
I could not

I cried to the Salvation Army
They offered to look after me and my baby
So I came back to the home
I was the lucky one

The Poem I Wrote In My Head

I wrote a poem in my head
To my daughter
"I want so much for time to stand still
Want to remember this moment forever

To etch the picture of your little face
Into the deep recesses of my mind
So I could retrieve it at my leisure
And never forget"

Staring out into the moonlight
Into the most beautiful picture
Ships and buoys lit up on the sea
And stars in the sky

Lights in the sea
Feel like stars were in my eyes
Or is it tears
When I look down at my baby

Lying in my arms   cont.

Giving you milk from the bottle
Feeling your little body all cuddly and warm
Looking at your little face

Wondering at the perfect little eye-brows
Exact replicas of my fathers
Feeling your little body all
Cuddly and warm
Looking at your little face

And your grey-blue eyes staring at me
So I spoke softly to her,
Whilst the rest of the house was sleeping
Told her about her granny and granddad

I never thought she would ever see
About not wanting to give her away
And I can still recall the feeling in my guts
The tightness in my throat
The tears filling up inside
The stitches still burning in my crotch
The fever in my head
And the sweat in my body

The moonlight over the lawn
And the stars over the sea
Time did stand still for us two
For that precious time

Wedding Day

All in a panic
And my heart is beating fast
Got to jump out of bed
And have a quick wash

Get everybody out of the way
I'm going to be late
Gonna get my hair done up especially nice
I'm getting married today   cont.

The hairdryers burning my head
Got to turn it down
This is taking far too long
They tug my hair ouch they're pulling the curlers
Out too fast

Waiting for a taxi
They've forgotten to pick me up
Marching through the town chain smoking
All the way
Got to hurry home again hair's all falling out

Everybody's waiting eyes shining
Presents lying on the floor
Have a smoke to calm me down
Today it's tasting really good

Is everybody ready
Taxi's at the door
Have you got the ring and everything
Only four minutes to go

Waiting outside the wedding doors
Got to wait outside
There are weddings going on in there
Do you know it's ours now and I'm the bride

Step inside the doors
Just you and me
Go over the lines a little please
I'm nervous you see

Now everybody's crowding in
To listen to our vows
Do you Clive take me next to you
To be your lawful wedded spouse

To Lucy

You are a precious treasure
That I could not give away
Someday I'll try to tell you
The tale of mystery
You were my own
Mine
And mine alone
And I fought to keep it so
You are my life
But you are not me
You are you
And I am but me
But without me
You would not been

I see the beauty in your face
Your curly locks of hair
Your eyes so grey
Your smile your laugh
One of gods miracles made in me
You cannot conceive
How life had seemed
When they tried to take you from me
Perhaps when you are old enough
Your story I shall tell
One day
When that day seems far away
When you can understand
It well

Lucy – Drive me crazy

I look at your face
And sometimes see a beautiful girl
And other times see a baby
And often see a five year old
Who tries to drive me crazy

Lucy - Wonder

I never cease to wonder
At the beauty in your face
Your eyes so full of laughter
Your smile the smile of grace

I never cease to wonder
At the games you like to play
Your little tricks and elfish grins
The dreamlands you create

Forever I'll sit and wonder
At the beauty in the world
And how god created a part for me
In the form of a little girl

Hiawatha and the Poets

Henry Longfellow
Sang his song of Hiawatha
Sailing down the shores of Gitche Gumee
Of his mother Old Nakomis
And his wedding to Minnehaha
And his death
And departure
To the land of the hereafter

Wordsworth penned
His spots of time
In The Prelude
Of his travels and his landscape
Of The Lake District
Of family and the Poor
Of a passing of a loved one
To the land of the hereafter

William Blake etched Heaven And Hell
And the Gates of Paradise

cont.

Of Jehovah's finger
Writing The Law
And walking among the stones of fire
And that Jesus wrote you will be born again
And the soul will sleep in the beams of light
In the land of the hereafter

Milton wrote his Paradise Lost
When he was blind
Of the fall of Satan
And of Man
And Adam and Eve
Wiping their tears
As they were expelled
To the land of the hereafter

Trace my skin

Take me on a journey of ecstasy and love
Carry me in folded arms and show me your love
Your kisses are petals falling onto skin
Your body is an envelope your lips seal me in

Trace my skin with gentle fingertips
Slowly slowly take your time it's ours alone
Send the fire to my breasts the fire love grows
Make them feel your hands caress make them throb

Lick them with your fiery tongue heat my chest
Suck them like you do a peach show me a caress
Trace a path deep deep down deep into my forest
Burn my trees burn my leaves find the secret passage

Place your magic wand at the open gate enter slowly in
Make our heated blood unite let the ecstasy begin

Kiss my face caress my breast drive up my tunnel of love
Start my honey flowing from its secret source

Lying in a bed of fire each second it burns more
Make your fire burn with mine make me yours   cont.

Breathe deeply breath slowly say you love me now
When your honey river joins with mine we'll overflow

I come to meet you on the road I'm coming along
If you hurry, we'll meet at the crossroads of loves song
A spark does fly a shock goes through your body shudders
We've come at last we've sealed again our love for each other

The Wedding in Bluebell Wood

I saw the wedding of the fairy queen
In a grove in bluebell wood
She sat on a pink rose petal throne
Her hair covered with rose buds
Holding her white robe of fairy lace
A primrose fairy stood behind
And waving yellow petal fans
Fairy bridesmaids stood in a line

And Puck played his magic flute
While the fairies sang songs of old
And they passed cups of cherry wine
In buttercups of gold

The handsome Prince of the laughing elves
Was to marry the fairy queen
He came marching through the bluebell paths
That were paved with golden leaves

His elfish pages followed
Holding his scarlet cloak
And the pixies did a sprightly dance
To the magic notes of the flute

The Prince sat next to his fairy queen
And took her hand in his
When the pixie priest came forward
With his bible made of leaves

He said a prayer and kissed their feet
cont.

And wished them lifelong bliss
Then the Prince of the elves gave his fairy queen
A lingering golden kiss

Twas the wedding of the fairy queen
A wondrous sight to watch
But when I woke twas only a dream
I dreamt in bluebell wood

Lost In an Ice-cream World

Hair the colour of sunshine
Curls cascading down her back
Dreamy look is in her eyes
So far away in a distant land
She looks like a princess in fairy land
Or an angel in the skies

Ice cream is in her hands
On her lips and in her hair
Ice cream is dripping down her chin
Ice cream getting everywhere
Little girl so sweet and fair

No she's sitting on a swing
Reaching up into the sky
Not aware of anything
Thinking of her Ice cream dream
Little angel in the clouds
Watching the world go by

Ode to a Snail

Once upon a time
There was this sad tale
Of Samson and Amy
The two little snails

cont.

One day Amy said to Sammy
Let's go for a short crawl
And find some juicy cabbage leaves
And have ourselves a ball

So they set off at a crawling pace
Right down the garden path
And found a juicy cabbage leaf
And tore it in half

But Sammy thought his half too small
And hit Amy on the head
And when he'd ate his cabbage leaf
He crawled off to his bed

But a Jackdaw spied poor Amy
Who was lying stunned in a buttercup
And down swooped the Jackdaw
And ate poor Amy up

So here ends this story
A sad little tale
And let it be a lesson
To all greedy snails

Such a Beautiful World

They are fighting in Ireland
They don't know why
And neither do I
They drop so many bombs
Shoot so many men
Ireland's rivers are full of blood
And it's such a beautiful world

They hijacked a train
Took everyone prisoner again
They pushed a man out
And shot him in the back
They don't know why and neither do I

cont.

Their babies on the train are crying
And it's such a beautiful world

They took guns inside a building
Because they wanted freedom
They blindfolded a little boy
Stuck a rope around his neck
And a gun in his back
He didn't know why and neither do I
And it's such a wonderful world
You can't go out for fear of a bomb
Can't take a ride for fear of a gun
Can't let your children out if your sight
Oh it's such a beautiful world

Sitting by a river

Sitting by a river
Under a Willow Tree
Watching the swans sailing on
Towards a sunsets mirror

Diamond sparkles onto a watery bed
Circles rippling whispers of a lover's honeymoon
Wild duck calling from the silvery reeds
First star appears above the beckoning trees

Moon is soon appearing to take over in the night
Sun is slowly sinking in a bath of blood red light
Stars come dancing in the night sky
Winking you their secrets laughing silently

Mother duck and her chicks retire to their bed
A nest of reeds welcoming sleep to sleepyheads
Water vole scurried to his home impatiently
The silent stillness descends upon the pond slowly

Night-time stillness rests
On a sleepy riverbed
Let's lean against our Willow Tree

cont.

And rest our weary heads

Mother nature will cover us
In her black blanket for the night
Moonlight and the stars so bright
Will be our bedside lamp

Hypocrite

You feel depressed
Cos, you only got bread
Think of those poor kids
Who are starving to death

So, you got a stomach ache
From eating too much food
What about the kid
Dying of a gunshot wound

So, you're really pissed off
Cos it's raining outside
Think yourself lucky
It's not bombs dropping from the sky

You read it in the papers
And you see it on the News
You say "those poor bloody babies"
"But there's nothing we can do"

Yes, you're a Hypocrite
And I'm a Hypocrite
And the whole goddam world
Is a Hypocrite

And they should give
The Victoria Cross
To all the innocent kids
Who lost

Fire Dreams

Sitting in the firelight pictures in your flames
Watching the crimson fairies playing games
Just having a smoke and dreaming again

In red hot cinders I see your coral caves
Your jewelled walls of rubies red
Where mermaids lie to rest their heads

Purples and whites greens and reds
Your colours dance in a burning bed
Of the fairies magic garden

See the fairies how they fly
From your burning fire to the sky
With wands of jewels flying by

Devils tongues of golden red and yellow
Fire of ages dancing in the grate
I sit mesmerised by your flames

Firelight pictures in my brain
Crimson fairies playing games
Having a smoke dreaming again

The Lady of Shalott

My Lady you are so peaceful
What ails thee sorely?
Pray tell me if you have the breath
What ails thee?

Your broken heart is aching
And your eyes are weeping
But yet you shed no tears
What ails thee?

Has your love departed thence

cont.

Has he gone before thee?
Closed the veil upon your eyes
What ails thee?

The reeds are whispering by the brook
You are slowly passing
Your eyes see not what is ahead
What ails thee?

No look of sadness have I seen
Save that within your eyes
The pain comes through your parted lips
What ails thee?

The water bears you down the stream
On this your last sea voyage
Your face it's full of such pity
What ails thee?

Christ's crucifix lies by your side
A friend to guide you
My Lady in your virgin gown
What ails thee?

Your ears they do not hear my words
Your eyes see nothing
Sad death awaits down yonder stream
For My Lady

Forest

In a moonlight clearing
The lovers unite
The wise old owl is watching
In his vigil of the night

The big tree spreads his arms
To overshadow their embrace
And the branches whisper secrets
In the moonlight place

cont.

The moon which is behind them
Silhouettes their darkened forms
As the lovers in the clearing
Caress till early morn

"My love I go to battle
You may not see me e'er again
My love I go to battle
For you I shall lament

I do not wish to leave you
Nor do I wish to die
I do not wish to leave you
Tomorrow I'll surely cry"

The moon was sadly watching
Their hearts were full of fear
The branches rustled in the moonlight
And the wise owl shed a tear

Turtle Soup

Hurry little turtle, hurry to the sea
The white waves are calling
Come, come to me
Break through your turtle egg and claw at the sand
Fight to get to the surface
As hard as you can

The vultures are waiting, waiting on the beach
Their evil eyes are watching
They want some turtle meat
Watch for the Iguana waiting in his tree
 And the Racoons are waiting
They all want you for tea

Hurry little turtle, hurry to the sea
The white waves are calling
Fight to be free
Across the beach to safety but watch for the crabs
With their band of armoured brothers   cont.

You wouldn't stand a chance
The waves are getting nearer the frigate birds are flying
They'll snatch you in their claws
And fly you to their hideout
The sharks are in the water waiting for prey
If you want to survive
Keep out of their way
Look little turtle look our to sea
The mother turtles are emerging
To lay eggs on the beach
Hurry little turtle don't get left behind
Your mother cannot see you
She'll squash you in the sand

Poor little turtle it's hard to survive
In a world full of enemies
And nobody's your friend
The fishermen are waiting out there in the sea
For the Lord Mayor of London
Wants turtle soup for tea

Rosco

Two Americans visited us
When we lived in North Road West
One was called Ian Gilroy
One was called Rosco

Rosco was a black American
And always had his hat on
He was AWOL from the army
Because of the war in Vietnam

I was pregnant at the time
Rosco was going to be godfather
To my baby
When she was born

But he disappeared
Maybe they "found" him
Maybe he was arrested   cont.

Maybe he had to go back to Vietnam

We never saw him again
But I have a picture of him
Holding Lucy, with his hat on
Rosco was a lovely man

I hope he didn't end up in Vietnam

Elusive Butterfly

Don't be concerned it will not harm you
It'd only me
pursuing something
I'm not sure of

Then another phones me
With the sad news
Bob died on Christmas day
All alone, found
found by his daughter

Now Bob pursues the butterfly
In Paradise
Bob my dear friend
Best of friends, till the end

You'd never hurt anyone
Except yourself
I threw dirt on your coffin
And saw Titch standing there

There were four of us
Bob and Jeff, Titch and me
Halcyon days for a long while
Until you found your habit

Pursuing something you were not sure of
Now you're a butterfly on the wing
Titch is in Cornwall I'm in Devon

cont.

And Jeff in as elusive as ever

When I first met him
He was with sweet Muna
An Indian "Princess"
I wonder if she knows Bob's flown

Goodbye Bob my friend
Maybe we'll meet again
On another plain
Some day in Paradise

Chips and Tartare Sauce

Suddenly got a craving for chips and tartare sauce
He just can't stop thinking of chips and tartare sauce
Just the thought of those chips makes his mouth water
And so he'll spend his last penny
On chips and tartare sauce
Walking in the freezing cold hands in pockets thinking hard
Of chips and tartare sauce
So with stars in his eyes he goes

Turning round the corner his nose begins to itch
That heavenly smell is coming
From those heavenly smelling chips
Asking for his goodies he can't wait to get outside

He hurriedly tears off the paper
To get to those beautiful chips
And tearing off the carton lid the tartare sauce does flow
Onto the chips waiting there to be eaten
Until his stomach's had its fill
Of chips and tartare sauce
Just dreaming
Of those chips and the tartare sauce

Rainy Day Blues

Storm
Thundering and lightening
Beating on the houses
Like a man in pain
It seems as if the world
Outside
is angry

Snow
Falling from the sky
Softly and silently
Like a dumb man's tears
It seems as if the world
Outside
Is silently crying

Wind
Howling through the trees
Moaning in the night
Like a woe-begotten child
It seems as if the world
Outside
Can hold its tears no longer

Rain
Dropping down the window
Sliding down the panes
Like tears down a cheek
It seems as if the world
Out there
Is full of pain

For after the storm
Came snow
After the wind came rain
As after the anger came tears
And after the tears came pain

Clouds

Your claim to fame
Was meeting Robbie Williams
At the rehab centre
For offenders
Alcohol was Robbie's
Poison
Charlie was yours

Robbie sang "Angels"
To you
Before it became a hit
In the charts
Clouds was in Wiltshire
You walked out of the joint
And escaped to Cornwall

You gave up on Charlie
And took up with another master
And moved to Devon with me
Knowing I would not forsake you
And with a lot of love
And affection
You began rehab again

With perseverance and patience
And always blessed with love
And protection
You got your life back
Now you're meeting up
With loving angels instead

Memory

With only my suitcase
And what was inside me
I walked through the doors
Into a strange place I did not know   cont.

Or care about
And knew only emptiness

Beginning To Learn

So you've started school
And you're on your own
Like a little lamb
Amongst a flock of sheep
They herd you through the doors

So you've started school
And you think it's fun
Will you still think that
In ten years to come
It's better that you choose

So you've started school
Begun eleven years
Of keeping still
Being told what is true
And what it's wrong to do

Well you've started school
You're growing up
Can't run to mum
You're on your own
A lamb amongst the sheep

Don't turn around
Walk through those doors
Your time has come
You can't walk back
The learning has begun

Another Poem

Sitting by a river
Under a willow tree
Watching the swans sailing on
Towards a sunsets mirror

Diamond sparkles onto a watery bed
Circles rippling whispers of a lovers honeymoon
Wild duck calling from the silvery reeds
First star appears above the beckoning trees

Moon is soon appearing to take over in the night
Sun is slowly sinking in a bath of blood red light
Stars come dancing in the night sky
Winking you their secrets laughing silently

Mother duck and her chicks retire to their bed
A nest of reeds welcoming sleep to sleepy heads
Water Vole scurries to his home impatiently
The silent stillness descends upon the pond slowly

Night-time stillness rests
On a sleepy riverbed
Let's lean against our Willow tree
And rest our weary heads

Mother Nature will cover us
In her black blanket for the night
Moonlight and the stars all bright
Will be our bedside lamp

Waiting To Be Born

I've a baby inside me
Less than an inch tall
A miracle inside me
Waiting to be born

cont.

Will it be a baby boy
Or a pink-faced little girl
Will she sleep peacefully
Or will he scream and bawl?
We're going to buy a tiny cradle
To welcome her home
A tiny wicker cradle
All of her very own

There's a baby inside me
Curled up in a ball
A tiny replica of you and me
So tiny and so small

I'll knit her little jackets
To keep her tiny body warm
we'll dress him like a little prince
From the day that he's born
We won't cut his locks
Until he's five years old
And then it'll be a trim
We'll let it grow long

There's a baby inside me
Waiting to be born
A baby formed from our love
And love she will be shown

She's got a tiny heartbeat
She's got a tiny brain
She's got such a tiny body
Just a tiny babe

We're going to have a baby
To join our family
A baby made from our love
And peace and security

There's a baby inside me
Less than an inch tall
A miracle inside me
Just waiting to be born

Phaedra

So peaceful and quiet
Lying there staring
What do you see
Do you see me?

Phaedra
At peace with the world
Looking around in silence
What goes on in your mind
What are your thoughts?

Phaedra
Your hair is so soft
Your eyes are so deep
Your perfect mouth
Lips so tender and small

Phaedra
A little baby, a bundle of love
There's peace in your eyes
And sunshine when you're smiling
The whole world is sad when it hears you crying

Phaedra
Beautiful baby
You came from Love
You are love
And we love you

Phaedra 2

With my baby inside me
Waiting to be born
We were watching Tangerine Dream
In The Guildhall
She was less than an inch tall

At home afterwards   cont.

In the warmth of the fire
We were searching for a name
In the Encyclopaedia Britannica
And came across - Phaedra

A part of their music
Was Phaedra
She could shorten it
When she was older
To Fay we thought

Meanwhile
Just waiting to be born
Was my baby Phaedra
Keeping warm
Less than an inch tall
Questions and Answers
By The Moody Blues
Was on the radio in the car
When I went into labour
In October

Phaedra arrived
On a Friday
"Loving and giving"
Still snug and so warm
Phaedra was born

Sucking two little fingers
And looking like her dad
In the morning
A sleepy bundle
Of Love
Questions and answers
By The Moody Blues
The answer to my prayers
As they sang in the song
And Phaedra was and is

Questions

You ask why that man
Hasn't got a beard
You ask why you can't have a cigarette
And why do we have to go to bed
At the end of every day
Why isn't the moon
Out with the sun
And why does the sky turn red
And where does the aeroplane go to
Why can't we buy money
And why do we eat bread
Why can't you go to work
To get money to buy sweets
Why do we have to wear
Shoes on our feet
In the street

You're a little girl
Who always demands
Answers to your questions
When you're a lady
You will find
Questions that CAN'T be answered

A broken dream

What would I be
Without you here
I'd be a dying fish
Stranded on the beach
Calling to the waves
Come back come back
I'd be a bird with a broken wing
Staring to the sky with tortured eye
I'd be a body without a soul
And my heart would scream
Come back, come back   cont.

As it shattered
A broken dream

Sleep Peacefully

Sleep peacefully little girl
Don't cry in your sleep
Give me a smile
From the corner of your mouth
So I know
You're having sweet dreams

Yellow Cloud

Yellow cloud on a moonlit night
Yellow cloud shining bright
Yellow cloud carry me on a sea of gold
Yellow cloud carry me to my home

Making Love

Making love
To you
Making love to me
Making love to you
Making love
On the dew
In the grass

Sun

The sun shone through the clouds
This morning
Like a smile

Like a smile through a veil
Like a smile from the eyes
Of a child

And then it went
Behind
And as I looked

It came out again
As if to say
It was still there

So that I knew
That the clouds would not stay
For ever

As love overcomes hate
And happiness misery
So it is with the sun

Overcoming the clouds
Life is full of clouds
But look closely

And you will find your sun
It's there - somewhere
It told me this morning

Sweet Child of Mine

Looking out at the sky
You said
"When I was a bird
I used to fly like that"

You said
"When you were little
I was your mummy"
You said it with such conviction

You still maintain that
That WAS the truth
And care for me
Like you ARE my mum

And now you are a mum
Of two lucky little girls
Of your own
I am so lucky to have you

Sweet Child of Mine

The Sixties and the Start of Revolution

The end of the Sixties
Start of the mystics
Magical mystery tour
The sunny summer of Love
And Peace

Flowers in the Rain
The beginning of Radio One
Scott McKenzie and his song
If you're going to San Francisco
Be sure to wear flowers in your hair

Make Love not War was on our lips
Protests against the war in Vietnam   cont.

Carnations were put inside the guns
At the Pentagon in the USA
But Martin Luther King was shot dead

Everyone wants to get high we sang
Love love love by the Beatles
Love is all around us by the Troggs
Ravi Shankar and George Harrison
And the emergence of Sitar music

The times they are a changing
Sang Dylan, Vocalists and Pacifists
And Trippy Hippies and Cannabis
And Happiness

It was a social revolution of long hair,
Mini skirts and hot pants, your fashion
Long dresses and Jesus sandals and passion
Wear what you want and be FREE
To live your dream

Hey Jude, Dock of the Bay
Born to be wild, Hello I love you
And Jimi Hendrix with Electric Ladyland
We were on a Magical Mystery Tour
Of Love not war
In the Sixties

Bushbaby

Lying on your side
With big sleepy eyes
Like a baby bush-baby
They look so wide

Staring at a flame
bewildered and amazed
to your bush-baby eyes
Everything's so strange

A smile on your face

cont.

Is sunshine every day   our bush-baby is love
In every way

The Sleeping Beauty

Slowly turn the handle
Tiptoe through the door
You're in the land of the sleeping beauty
Lying in a sleeping room
Quietly don't breathe a word now
Sleeping beauty's fast asleep
In her golden dream world sailing
On a sea of simplicity
In a picture book of fairy tales
lying on a lily flower
In a pool of moonlight shining
Lies the sleeping beauty still
Quietly don't breathe a word now
Tiptoe out the door
Don't wake the sleeping beauty
Or she might shed a tearating

Pink Dog Dream Part One

Running round in circles
Can't be seen
Round and round the room
Guilty minds running round
Walking the hill up and up
Trying take the coat off
Jealous minds jealous eyes
Watching staring
Footsteps angry faces
Running down the hill
Stop stop come back
Can't stop running running
Hiding on the bed   cont.

Can't light the cigarette
Shaking hands angry faces
Voices shout get out stop
Asking questions
Nothing nothing done
Leave me won't stop you
Walk by the wall
Look at the water
School bus children
Climb on the bus
Take me far away
Back seat children
Legs on the seat
Voices laughing talking
End of the road

Pink Dog Dream Part Two

Look through the window
Mongol children backs bent staring
At the sky
You are behind waiting
On the road
You cut your hair growing bald
Get me off this bus
Children pushing bus starts
Jump off
Your arms hold a child
Thank goodness that's over
Walk back up the road
Pink dog standing
On his hind feet
Talking dogs talking
Big dogs small dogs
Surrounding pink dog
Dogs around me
Dogs attack me
Talking dogs disappear
Walking home
Kitchen   cont.

I'll have Albran in a soup bowl
Open eyes
Only a dream
Only a dream

Nobody but Me

I sit here talking to nobody
Everyone talking to someone except me
I feel so peaceful but they break the silence
 I don't feel any part of this and want to leave
Maybe I'm not here though everyone else is
Everyone else is talking everyone else is here
Someone talks to me and breaks into my shell
Of peace and nothingness

I cannot answer no words will come
And soon they are gone and I wonder
If they ever were here
Or if I imagined those voices and figures
And now I sit here
So quiet talking to nobody
Nobody talking to me
For there is nobody here but me

City

Rooftops
Dirty grey slabs
Iron gutters
Broken windows

Scraggy cat
Walks along
Slowly
Carefully
So as not to step
On broken glass

cont.

Cries
Stops
And licks her paws

No food
No milk
No home

Pavement
Dirty dustbins
Iron railings
Broken bottles

Poor old tramp
Stumbles on
Miserably
Silently
And looks around
For shelter
From the rain
Pauses
And strokes his beard

No food
No drink
No home

Poor creatures
In this city
Knowing no love

Taro

Born at home on my bed
My little man
Feeling your little warm body
On mine

Beautiful blond--haired brown-eyed boy
Often mistaken for a girl   cont.

Took you to the barbers shop
You cried tears when it was cut

Musical from the start
Superstar on the guitar
And the keyboard
Tapping your feet to the beat

You didn't like school
Or the rules
And got expelled
When you burnt their books

Made up for everything
When Alan died
At the hospital
When confronted with his dead body

You visit me
To check I'm okay
Make me laugh
When I'm down

Wrote me poems
"When you're all stressed
Remember
You're the best"

Love you

Glastonbury with Taro

Glastonbury festival
A magical spectacle
Bought the tickets
And packed our bags
And we were ready for off
Got the bus as far as we could go
Thousands of others
Hitching a ride

cont.

Got a lift to the site
Found family and friends
To share a tent with
And slept ready for the morning

Kids at the play area had flick knives
Not the friendly hippie kids I remembered
Taro found a friend to play around with
So I could chill with the music
Rock and Roll and all things cool
Beautiful happy people having fun

Time to go home now following the crowds
Got to Glastonbury town and a bus found
Taro slept all the way back
Two sleepy heads came home

Wooden Heart Played by Taro

Can't you see I love you
Please don't break my heart in two
Cause I don't have a wooden heart
Remember

You playing a keyboard
At The Holiday Inn
For Elvis
And everyone watching
You're an Artist
Won a prize for your lighthouse
Your teacher was so proud
But you don't like the spotlight

You were the fastest runner in school
Until you were disqualified
For swearing
At the teacher

Said I love you so much mum
When I grow up

cont.

I'll read bedside stories to you
Cos I don't have a wooden heart

Friendship

My ears are sore my throat is sore
My mouth is full of ulcers
My doctor gave me two weeks off
To get better from I don't know what
What is to be, what is to come
To find my equilibrium

Funny how friends make you aware
When you think you've had enough
Aware that they are there
And come up with an answer
You wouldn't have found
If they hadn't been around

First Night

You came up to see me
Wanted to know all about me
The people I'd been with
And loved

Went in the Dolphin
Walking back I asked
To hold your hand
It felt right

First night on passion
"I'll give us ten years" you said
I thought it would be
A one night stand
You'd always been interested in me
You said, but didn't know why

cont.

I'd always fancied you
But never thought I'd have you

We're still together
Nearly twenty five years later
And I'll always love you
Even though you're gone

Brentor Church

We walked into Brentor Church
One morning
It was empty of people
The marriage ceremony had been left open
On the altar
I was looking at it
"Is that for us" You said

We smiled
And as St Michael looked on
We married each other
Just us, together
Using our own rings
The turquoise one you'd just bought
In Tavistock

It felt magical
Like we were meant to be
We felt special
And lucky
To be alive
And together
Forever

It was many years later
At your funeral
That I told the story
Of our marriage ceremony
At Brentor church
To a packed congregation

cont.

So many came, it was standing room only

And a black cat
Jumped onto your coffin
At the graveside
RIP beautiful man
And thank you
For the memories
And your love

Jain

Jain was a friend of mine
Went to live
In Portugal
But came back
With Cancer

After the chemotherapy
And the radiotherapy
She decided to live
In the countryside in Cornwall

We tried everything
To keep her alive for longer
Crystal healing
Colour therapy, massage

The doctor said
Cannabis is good for Cancer
So we bought loads and buried it
In the garden

We went back to Portugal
While she was still able
And when the weather was hot
We ate fresh Apricots from the tree

Back in Cornwall
They gave her
The Endorphin of Morphine cont.

To take away the pain

I played her the song
You've got a friend
As she lay there dying
You've been great Mary she said

You've been great Jain I said
Where you're going
There'll be no more pain
Jain

How would you like friends to remember you Jain
I said
I'd like people to smile when they remember me
She said

Come Again Jain

September ninety-three
Jain left us
October ninety-three
I dreamt of Jain last night
In the kitchen
With me and Jain and others
And I wanted to say
How come you're dead?
But you can still be with us
But I couldn't say it
In case she didn't know
And Dave was watching us
So I talked of something else
But it was lovely
To see you Jain
Come again

Away From It All

Washed the nappies
Cleaned the pans
Now I can sit down
And read Alice in Wonderland

Serendipity

I was sat at my computer ready for work
You came over and kissed me
What happened to us you said
You kept taking heroin I said
They watched as you walked away

We'd been together a long time
I'd put up with your habit
Which you could not give up
So you lived in the caravan
While I lived in my place

You were doing rehab
They knew this at work
So they offered counselling
While they kept an eye on us
And put us on different shifts
They knew we loved each other
Knew what we were going through
It took a long time
For you to give up the habit
You were taking it right from the start
Eventually you saw the light
You said I was the light
At the end of your tunnel
When we got together
Now you'd realised

You'd said it was your friend
It's not your friend I said
It's a habit you've got to kick

cont.

Away
From you

So you did, eventually
Finally realising it was up to you
That you had to conquer it
And you went through with it
The sweating, shivering madness

And we loved each other again
Travelling the world
Laughing and smiling
Enjoying what we had
Together again

And then you died

Bible on Our Shoulders

Arriving after our flight from Switzerland
We walked into a park
In San Francisco
When a friendly American smiled at us
"I see you have the bible on your shoulders"
A fine welcome to San Francisco

Memories of San Francisco

Sitting on the beach
Looking over to Alcatraz
And Golden Gate Bridge
Sleeping in the sleaziest
Down Town San Francisco hotel
Where they had iron bars around reception
They were making deals on the phone
We asked the way
Oh he said
You need the Haight Ashbury district

cont.

Riding a San Francisco street car
We bought a frisbee
With Haight Ashbury on it
Still have it years later
Golden Gate Park
Long haired hippies were still there
After all these years
We played frisbee flying to the skies
You wrote a postcard to a friend
While I made a joint on the grass

Some guy gave us paper green roses for our hair
Still got the photo of you
I got cactus thorns in my backside Ouch!
Kicking a fir cone around the park till it got dark
And we lost our way
Met up with Demitree our friend
Staying in an upmarket hotel
Hearing sirens in the night
A nice guy opened up his shop
So we could get our photos developed

Finding a shop selling Red Indian dolls
We bought the cup
That says
Fuck you you fucking fuck
I planted some seeds
In Golden Gate Park
We saw in the New Year
And said goodbye
To San Francisco
Before we caught the aeroplane home

Watching the Druids at Stonehenge

We camped in Wiltshire and drove
To Stonehenge; mysterious
Magical Sacred Stonehenge
And waited for the Ceremony

The Druids came in a majestical line
Dressed in white robes
The Eldest Druid wearing gold

cont.

Walking around the Colossal stones

The Megaliths; the Sarsen Stones
And the Blue Stones
Transported from afar
From Maenclochog in Wales

Stones aligned with the Summer Solstice
For the Sunrise
And the Winter Solstice
For the Sunset

The flowers of the Druids
The Meadow Sweet flower
And Vervaint and Water Mint
And Mistletoe the Aphrodisiac

The Celtic love knot
The Tree of Life and The Green Man
The Bardic Teaching, creative power
Revered by all the Druids

We merely watched in awe
When we saw the Druids perform
Their Ceremony
At Stonehenge

Budleigh Salterton

In fine weather we'd drive to Budleigh Salterton
A little town on the Jurassic Coast
For the Cream Tea we liked the most
In the Dolphin cafe

But before entering the town we'd go for a spell
To Shillingford Woods to see the bluebells
Where we were decidedly spellbound as we sat
In swell haze of a blue hue

Then off to the cafe for the Cream Tea   cont.

With tea for you and coffee for me
And an extra scone if we were hungry
Before we left for the sea front

The Red Cliffs of Budleigh also famous
Are the oval quartz pebbles on the beach
And the painting "The boyhood of Raleigh"
And of course Raleigh was born near here

But the smell of the sea and the waves
Excel - sometimes the waves are red
Churned up by the sand, and the noise of sea
And the pebbles on the beach is all magic to me

And driving home in the sunset
What more can you need

Bus Station in Mexico

The longest coach journey ever
San Francisco to Mexico
By Greyhound Bus
Traumatically frisked for drugs
We alighted in Tijuana
Massive bus station
All speaking Mexican
We didn't speak

An official caught us
Looking confused
Took us into his office
We did not speak Mexican
He did not speak English
It was difficult communicating
He thought I was a government official
He drove us to a hotel and left us there

Hotel was plush very plush
The local Mexicans were poor very poor
Weather was hot hot hot   cont.

It was Christmas Eve
The bank was open
All the cops had guns
We went to the supermarket
Could not decipher the writing

Christmas Day in Mexico
Eating salad
Drinking orange juice
Out in the park all the kids had bikes
For Christmas
Tiny squirrels scampering all over
We phoned England
Happy Christmas from Mexico

Travelling Around Europe

Freedom from work
Redundancy money to hand
We bough a campervan
And caught the ferry, me and my man

Settling for a campsite in France
We found a secret garden on our travels
And canoed down the river
Accompanied by Herons and Storks
Then on to Yverdon-Les-Bains
In Switzerland
With fields of sunflowers and mountains to climb
And a picnic by the lake

In the Czech Republic
We found a little house to rent
With a friendly landlady living next door
Who supplied us with meat and all we could eat

Came to Poland and Auschwitz
Saw the mountains of hair, combs and shoes
Man's inhumanity to man
And the suffering of the Jews

cont.

Met Zorro For Peace in the streets
Of Amsterdam
Saw Van Gough and the Diamante Museum
And the Bulldog coffee shop before we left

Arriving in Denmark
They told us "Don't feed the Pigs"
As they rented us a luxurious apartment
In Art Deco style

We explored Kolding Castle
And were told the history of the Vikings
As we sailed on Kolding Lake
On boats made of swans

On to Germany
Where a poster told us
Life is short live your dream
And share your passions

We did

The Magic of Pamukkale and Konya

Cascading white waters looking like snow
Walking barefoot up and down the terraces
Warm healing waters made of calcium
Sodium sulphate magnesium and Iron
Warmed our feet

Ye gods worshipped by Greeks and Romans
Great Apollo healing us gave us poetry
Sister Artemis of the moon and wild nature
Poseidon sent earthquakes from the sea
While Pluto slept in his underworld

While we bathed in Cleopatra's Pool

Mineral rich Karahaynt in the neighbourhood
Had Iron in her waters with metal oxide

cont.

Turning her terraces red green and yellow
Healing the heart, skin and diseases
In Anatolia

Travelling to Konya on a motorbike
Up a mountain in the moonlight
It was a long way up but we made it to the top
And we saw the city beneath our feet
Huge, massive, in the shadow of the moon

A hotel with pictures of Whirling Dervishes
Welcomed us tired travellers with Halva
A guide took us around the Mosque
After taking off our shoes, to tell us the history
Of Konya
A Turkish flag waved to us from the hillside
As we made the journey back
To Bodrum where you bought me my ring
Of sapphire blue and after a swim in the pool
We waved our goodbyes to Turkey

The Viking Festival of Fire

Abby was a good friend of mine
And bought a house in The Shetlands
Come up and see me she said
And stay for the Viking ceremony

So up in the snow I go
To "Up Helly Aa"
It's very cold in the Shetlands
On a Tuesday in January

All dressed up in Lerwick
Vikings and Valkyries
Jarl with his Raven Winged Helmet
And his Axe with Runes on his sword

Guizer Jarl the Norseman played the lead
And they all drank their sparkling Mead

cont.

And, intoxicated, they sang along to the tune
Of "The Norseman's Home"

The seafaring Shetland islanders
Descended from the Scandinavians
Were illuminated by a torch-lit procession
As a thousand of them went down to the water

The Viking longboat awaited
And the fire was lit and thrown
And caught alight, a magnificent sight
The splendour of it mesmerising my eyes

It's been many years since
But the memories remain
And I hope to see you
In Valhalla
My love

The Palestinian Genocide

Children stumble
Over the rubble
After the devastation
Of invasion

In the hospital
They perform operations
But are denied proper medication
While Polio strikes them down

Where is Peace?
Starvation
Is Salvation
To the dead and dying

Jerusalem
In the shadow of the cross
Confronts wickedness
While Jesus weeps

cont.

Bibi is a Hebrew
Who pursues
His "God-given right"
To kill the Arab Jews in Gaza

They're bombing the Golan Heights
Where the Druze mourn
All forlorn
Destruction of the Jews and Arabs

The International Court of Justice
Condemn the decade long
Occupation of Israel
As Unlawful

The Al Jazeera News
Talk of the negotiations
Of who blames Hezbollah
And who blames Hamas
And who blames Israel for sending the bombs
And who blames the children for throwing the stones
While the children stumble
Over the rubble

And who blames Hamas
And who blames Israel

The Samaritans

I completed my training
And became a Samaritan
Mainly just sitting
And listening
To very sad souls

The majority were young girls
Who cut themselves
They said it gave them
A feeling of release
From pain   cont.

The majority of girls
Had been abused
By their fathers
Or uncles
Or grandfathers
Or even brothers

Then there were phone-calls
By Men
The majority whose mums had died
And they didn't want to live
Without them

Then there were the ones
Who wanted to kill themselves
Right there and then
While they were on the phone
Ready to die

I had one who was in the attic
Had a noose around his neck
With the phone in his hand
Wanting to end it all
A taxi driver who had lost his license

I asked him if he had someone
In the family he could talk to
To tell his troubles to
If he'd get down from the attic
He said he could talk to his brother

And so he took the noose off his neck
And left the attic
I'd talked him out of it
It's a hard job being a Samaritan
Heart-breaking

But you felt good on the way home
Knowing you'd done someone some good
Helped someone in need
And there's a lot of needy people
Out there, in this god-forsaken world

Masterpieces of Art in Europe

I'd like to travel
Around Europe
And see some real Art
Would you like to come?

I'd start in Spain
And see Picasso's painting
Of Guernica about the second world war
Would you like to see that?
I'd like to go to Spain and Barcelona
And see Salvador Dali's painting
Of Sleep and The Resistance Of Memory
How about that?
I'd like to go to France
And see The Bayeux Tapestry
About the Norman invasion of England
Would you like to see it?

I'd like to go to Italy, to Florence
And see Michelangelo's sculpture of David
And the Birth of Venus emerging from her shell
Would you like that?

I'd like to go to Milan
And see Leonardo Da Vinci's painting
Of The Last Supper
Would you be interested in that?

I'd like to go to Norway
And see The Scream by Edvard Munch
As well as his painting of Madonna
Will you come?

I'd like to go to Austria
To see Gustav Klimt's The Kiss
And his muse Emilie in Vienna
I'd really enjoy that, would you?
I'd love to go to Holland, to Amsterdam
And see Van Gough's paintings of
A Starry Night, Sunflowers and Irises   cont.

Would you come with me?

 I'd like to go to London
To see Claude Monet's Water Lilies
In The National Gallery
Would you accompany me?

Or is this just a fanciful
Reality
And just a daydream
Of what I'd really like to do?
Before we go home to our reality

Climate Change

There were volcanic eruptions
In Iceland today
Causing the Earth to tremor
As red and gold rivers erupted
From the volcano
Spewing rivers of blood
Down the mountain

They tell us Chad is the most vulnerable
Place on Earth, and the hottest
Where Lake Chad is drying up
Where they suffer floods
And draughts and plagues
And is surrounded
By the Sahara Dessert

There's flooding in Africa;
Kenya, Burundi, Somalia
And Tanzania
There are wild fires in Europe,
Portugal and Greece
With loss of life
And evacuations

There are bush fires in Australia

cont.

With extreme drought
With wild fires in Canada
And Hawaii and Russia,
In Kazakhstan and Mongolia
South Sudan and Nigeria
And in Chile with death to life

And then there's Starvation
Because of displaced people
And destroyed farmland
And they tell us
That Iceland is the safest place to live
 To avoid being affected
By Climate Change
But they tell us not to worry
Because wind and solar energy
Outnumber fossil fuel today
And that's a healthy remedy

Rhubarb and Mustard

We used to meet at the cafe in the morning
Before I went swimming and you went walking
For a coffee and a chat
We were regulars in Rhubarb and Mustard
When it was fine we sat outside
They were used to seeing us together
One day we'd both worn our Looe T-shirts
Not knowing we were both going to wear them
"You know what that means?" she said "No"
"You're in love" We smiled because we were

One day I was sat outside on my own
"On your own?" she said questioningly
I sighed "He died"
"Well I never expected that" she said
"Neither did I" I said
So now I go there on my own before swimming
They're always very friendly in there
I showed them my poem "The dawn of Creation"   cont.

They liked it
And gave me a free cake to take home

Shelly and Kahlil

Romantic Shelley
Loved love, reason and progress
He wrote To a Skylark,
In the golden lightning of the sunken sun
My name is Ozymandias, King of Kings
And I met a traveller from an antique land
Prometheus - he was the champion of mankind
And through Elysian garden islets he went
And said to the West Wind
O Wild West Wind you're a wild spirit
I love love said Shelley
Though he has wings to flee

Such a pity he drowned
On his way home to his love

Kahlil Gibran
Was a poet
Who also loved love
He said of love
When love beckons to you
Follow him

He was asked to talk about children
And said, your children are not your children
They are the sons and daughters
Of Life's Longing
Love talks to you so that you may know
The secrets of your heavens

Be like a running brook
That sings its melody
To the night
And let the winds of the heavens
Dance between you
Insha-Allah

The Impressionists

Monet first started Impressionism
Setting up rows of easels
To catch the changing light of day
while painting his Haystacks in Giverny

He set up his Musee de l'orangerie
To paint his masterpiece of Water-lilies
Covering all the walls
But lost his sight and died before he finished

His life-long friend was Renoir
Famed for his lunch at the boating party
Cezanne painted skulls and card players
While Degas painted his ballet dancers

And Pessario painted Paris
And the Boulevard Montmartre
And Gauguin painted his two Tahitian Girls
In the South Seas

Seurat painted a Sunny Sunday afternoon
On the banks of the Seine with can can dancers
Showing the provocative embodiment
Of bourgeois decay

While Van Gough painted Agnostina
His friend and his lover, in the nude
He drank like a fish and lost his teeth
Painting The Green Fairy before he went insane

The Impressionists were geniuses
Rebelling against classical subject matter
Creating works of art of their own magic
That reflected the world as they saw it

Anne Franks Diary

Anne was born in Frankfurt, Germany
And moved into the secret annex
In Amsterdam with her family

Anne's diary was a birthday present
She called her diary Kitty
Kitty was a friend she could talk to

With sister Margot, mother Edith and father Otto
And the Van Daans and Mr Dussel
They lived in silence during the day, only talking at night
Until they were betrayed and arrested
And taken to the police station and redirected
To Auschwitz Concentration Camp

Anne, sister Margo and their mother
Were devastated neglected and dejected
Then Edith died in Auschwitz from starvation

Anne and Margot were transferred to Bergen-Belsen
Where the filth the wet and the cold made them sick
And they both caught and died from the Typhus

Anne had begun her diary when she was thirteen
She died in Bergen-Belsen when she was fifteen
But her spirit shines through in her diary

"I don't think of all the misery but of the beauty
That still remains" Your light shines on Anne

The Golden Stool of Asante

King Osei Tutu
Received the Golden Stool
From Heaven
Many moons ago

cont.

And King Osei Bonsu inherited it

From the Rain Forests in the Ivory Coast
The Asante tribe came to pay homage
With their colourful umbrellas
And their Gold
To their King

The Asante was a huge nation
Before the British came
"The rainbow is around every neck
Of every nation"
Was the Asante proverb
Their streets were full of Gold
And they sifted the earth
For loose Gold-dust
After the ceremonies
Were over

Craftsmen, with virtuosity and patience,
Made the Asante's Gold regalia:
Long staffs wrapped in Gold foil,
And Gold handled elephant tail whisks
To whisk away evil

The ceremonial war helmet
  Worn by the King
Was made of antelope skin
With golden jaws and trophy heads
Trimmed with Gold

The King received well wishes
With whom he shared palm wine
From a gourd covered in stripes of Gold
And Silver, while guards stood by
With Gold handled swords

The British caused a war
Deposed the King of the Asante nation
Called the country GHANA
And auctioned the gold relics in London
The elephant tail whisks hadn't worked

Mary Elizabeth Down

Volodymyr and Vladimir

Volodymyr was chosen democratically
By the people of Ukraine
Because of what he stood for:
Anti-establishment and anti corruption

Vladimir inherited his position
As acting president of Russia
Whether his people like it or not
The Russian people didn't have a choice
Volodymyr Zelensky
Won his election
By a landslide
Vladimir Putin
Had a law degree
And belonged to the KGB

Zelensky had a law degree
And united his people
against Putin
And his 'special military operation'
To take Ukraine
By force and subordination

Putin has China and North Korea
On his side
Zelensky has the rest of the world
Behind him
The Ukrainian soldiers
Fight for what they believe in

A food crisis developed
Ukraine supplies most of the world's wheat
Putin stole it from the boats
And put it in the global granary
Resulting in food insecurity
For the rest of the world

Sanctions were imposed on Russia
Amid word-wide condemnation
The men of Ukraine go to war

cont.

Mothers and children are now refugees
Taken in by other countries who form an alliance
While the men fight on to save them from the aggressors

Power struggles all over the world
While the people fight their battles
And the children inherit
The perils of the master races
As they try to make sense
of what they are faced with

The Island of Corfu

An island in Greece in the Ionian Sea
The crystal blue sea
A haven for you and for me
Was Corfu

With sandy beaches too hot to walk on
We hired two quod bikes
To explore the island on
Driving to the beaches in the sun

We found a little boat
On the shore just waiting for us
Found a cafe with a hammock to lie in
And different coloured chairs to sit on

With games to amuse us
Chess and draughts and dominoes
And I was playing backgammon
While you ate sandwiches of salmon

After exploring the olive groves
We returned to our apartment
With a veranda and our balcony haven
Before we caught the aeroplane home

Vlissingen and John-Robbie

We met in The Spinning Wheel
In Vlissingen
John-Robbie was the bartender
"Will you be my girl and I'll be your man?"

He was going to see the Stones
The next day
Asked if I'd like to go
With him

Rolling Stones Voodoo Lounge
Rotterdam
Open-air
The excitement made me faint

They opened with "Satisfaction"
It felt like I'd waited all my life
To hear that live on stage
With Mick Jagger in front of me

Two years later
Back to Rotterdam
To see Neil Young
And Alanis Morissette

And a night out
At the best night club
In Amsterdam
The Milky Way

He bought me the Rod Stewart CD
A spanner in the works
And played it to me so much
So that I could remember all the words

And he taught me the Dutch words
For I love you
"Ik hou van jou"
John-Robbie

The Ladies Who Sang the Blues

Joan Armatrading - the British singer
Sang with love and affection
And a lot of dedication
Her own version
Of folk and jazz and rock and roll

Dorothy Moore sang the Blues her way
It was her haunting rendition
Of "Misty Blue"
I loved the best of all she could do
One of the best female singers of the Blues

Etta James known as the Matriarch of the Blues
Sang her version of "I'd rather go blind"
Her version is the best you can find
She won herself a place
In the Hollywood Hall of Fame

Roberta Flack was a Soul Singer
Born in the Black Mountains of California
Her song "Killing me softly with his smile" won her a Grammy Award
"The first time ever I saw your face" embraced
Her love of sweet Soul music

Janice Joplin Queen was the Queen of Rock and Roll
"Maybe" was the song she sang with Soul
She gave her all to rock and roll
Had a voice that none could beat
On the streets, of New York

Billie Holiday Queen of Jazz
Famous for her song "Strange Fruit"
The song of the century by Time Magazine;
A protest song showing she was the Cream of Jazz
And of The Civil Rights Movement in the USA

She sang with feeling "Lover come back to me"
U2 wrote their song "Angel of Harlem";
A tribute to Billie, who they knew
As their "Lady Day with Diamond Eyes   cont.

Magnified"

They were all the Ladies Of The Blues
Who sang their songs their own way
Songs of Blues and songs of the Soul
And songs of Rock and Roll
And all that Jazz

Che Guevara

Born in Santa Fe in Cuba
Died in Bolivia
A Revolutionary symbol of Rebellion
To the very end

At eleven years old
Che was throwing stones
With the street urchins
In solidarity with strikers

At twelve years old
Che met Sigmund Freud and became his friend
in 1955 he met Fidel Castro in Mexico City
And began his campaign to overthrow
The regime of the Cuban Dictator Batista

Appalled by poverty hunger and disease
Che trained the peasants to fight for Liberty
And against corruption by the Bolivian
And American military and the CIA

Hounded by his enemies,
His wasted and bullet-ridden body
Was peppered with gunshot wounds
But he died with a single shot to the heart

The cameraman immortalised Che
The fallen champion, for the newspaper,
Cosmetically enhancing his face
And his hands were cut off at the request

cont.

Of a government minister in La Paz
A cast being made of them as a desk ornament

Protests against his death took place
Throughout the world, pictures of a smiling Che
Appeared in London and Paris
Protests took place from Algeria to Angola

Candles were lit in Budapest and Prague
Che t-shirts were worn in Protest Marches
By students emulating his style of dress
With military fatigues and berets

Che was a poet warrior and a diarist
Able to yield the pen and a submachine gun
With equal skill, and his memory lives on
A Martyr to Marxism

John Mayall Died Today

John
Did you see The Bear
When you went on location
To Laurel Canyon?

Did you send the blue fox
Home again
To go Back To The Roots?

Did you look in the mirror
And start walking
On Bare Wires?

Have you ever loved a woman
But wished you were mine
When you sang Primal Solos?

Did you hide away
From Tucson Lady
When you became The Last Of The British Blues   cont.

Did you find "Another Kinda Love"
When you were living alone
On A Hard Road

Did you say "Why worry"
When you were in Mexico City
Singing The Road Show Blues?

Did you find Room To Move
In California
When you came to the turning point?

Did you feel Supernatural
When sitting in the rain
Writing The World Of John Mayall?

Did you find a wild new love
With a gypsy lady, when you decided
There would be no more interviews?
In reply John said
"The time is right for a new direction"
- In heaven, John?

I Say Hello Beautiful Man

I say "Hello, beautiful man"
And "Where did you go?"
To your picture
Every morning

I read a saying from your box of tricks
Before I put my make-up on
And tell you what the weather's like
Every day out in the garden

I talk to you and tell you how I'm doing
How everyone is doing
How the world's in a mess
As usual

cont.

I say goodnight to you
When I lay down to sleep
While Mona Lisa looks on
Silently

We Had It All

We had it all didn't we
We had love you and me
It was like a dream
An amazing stream
Of love

Sealed with a kiss
A feeling of bliss
We said we'd be together
And stay together forever
In love

We travelled in Sunlight
And bathed in Moonlight
We made each other smile
And took the time for a while
To savour it

We travelled England with a caravan
Then travelled Europe in a campervan
We flew to Africa in an aeroplane
Got a ferry to Rotterdam
We circled the world

We had it all

Mohammed Ali

"I float like a butterfly
And sting like a bee
I am the greatest
I'm Mohammed Ali"

He fought Sunny Liston
The Thriller in Manilla
He fought George Foreman
In the rumble in the jungle
"If my mind can conceive it
And my heart can believe it
Then I can achieve it
I am the Concord of boxing you see"

Ali refused the draft to go to war
He challenged the US government
That the war in Vietnam was a genocide
Was sent to jail, gave up boxing for a while

He got in the ring with Tom Jones
Who gave him a left jam
And a right cross
And called him Trigger

He was friends with Michael X
And took him to see Sonny Liston
And watched him beat him
Until they fell out over religion

He said to Jimmy when he had chemo
"I'm gonna beat George Foreman
And you're going to beat Cancer"
In the Pensilvania hospital

Jimmy said "I'm gonna meet God
And tell him I'm a friend of Mohammed Ali
And will prepare a better place for him
In heaven where I'll be"

"Don't count the days but make the days count   cont.

I wasn't just a good father I was King of the world
And I'm the greatest fighter of all time"
He said in his book 'The Soul of a Butterfly'

Sri Lanka

Sacred Temple OF THE TRUTH
Drinking fresh Pineapple juice
Good and bad luck
Rescued by a Tut-Tut

Memories of Sri Lanka

I had my wallet stolen by boys
On the train
We missed our stop
Got out at Mount Lavinia
In the dark
The Tut-Tut man drove us home

Rode an elephant
Held snakes
Coiling round our necks
Visited the Hindu Temple
But The Sacred Tooth
Was hidden from us

Visited the Urang Utang
Hairy scary staring eyes
While the White Tiger
Paced up and down
Up and down and up and down
And the Giant Tortoise sat with the Leopard

Witnessed a beautiful Indian wedding
At the Pegasus Reef Hotel
While a drone in the sky took photos
And, in our hotel room,
The pillows were sculptured swans

And on the beach
You ate an ice cream   cont.

While the sun set
And the Sri Lankan boys
Taking their rods went fishing
They were the most wonderful sunsets

Ever seen

Over the Rainbow

Where did you go?
I want to go up to Brentor church with you again
I want to go to Italy with you again
I want to go to San Francisco with you again
I want to go to Budleigh Salterton with you again
Where did you go?
I play 'Over The Rainbow' on your mouth organ
(I'm getting better at it)
Have you gone over the rainbow?
Why oh why can't I?
I miss you
So much
So very very much
I love you

My Marilyn Monroe Bag

The elderly gentleman said to us: I just don't want to wake up in the morning
She said to him "we're here to help you live
Not to die
"But I've got nothing left to live for...
And the state of the world as it is now well..."
So I talked to him for a while to take his mind
Off it... he was from Scotland... been away from it
For a very long time

We got his bed ready for him and he pushed himself to the bathroom with the
help of his walking frame - very slowly cont.

An old lady said to me: "I went to my doctor today and he gave me more pills to stay alive...
But why?"
And we both looked out of the window -
Not knowing what to say when I left
Every time she squeezed my hand, gently
And gave a sweet smile

I helped an old lady get out of bed - it took two of us because she'd had a stroke - one held her head while the other held her feet and we'd turn her round so we could help her off the bed into her walking frame. And then she walked with it over to the commode. She never said a word - since she'd had a stroke she had lost the power of speech - so she smiled with her eyes and nodded with her head

"She never complains" says her husband - well that's obvious I thought, since she can't speak

One nice old lady was from London - 'Are you a Cockney?" I said "Yes I am - are you from London?" "No, I said, but my mum was" "Oh what part?" she said "Ealing" she was impressed looked a bit sad; "I was from the poorer area - Highgate Cemetery - but I had a lot of bad things happened to me and ended up in Plymouth - do you like Marilyn?" she said - looking at my bag
Some of them had Alzheimers, some of them Dementia; but they all had something in common -

They all liked my Marilyn Monroe bag;
"some like it hot" one said "Isn't that Marilyn" said another - yes, they all recognised Marilyn - and it always made them smile

A tribute to Leonard

I heard Leonard today - talking
Of his song, the sisters of Mercy
Who are not departed or gone
But Leonard is
Like a bird on a wire -
No more

Take this waltz, take this waltz he cried
From a concert hall in Vienna -   cont.
Take this waltz, take this waltz

85

It's yours now - it's all there is

Like Suzanne who fed you tea and oranges
That came all the way from China
He fed us songs and poetry that came
All the way from Canada

He said to Hank Williams how lonely does it get -
In the Tower of song?
Hank never answered him but he heard him
Coughing all night long

Suddenly the night has grown colder -
Alexandra's leaving with Leonard on her shoulder
Say goodbye to Alexandra leaving
Then to Leonard and our loss

So long Marianne - and Leonard - it's time
That we began to laugh
And cry and cry - and cry about it all
Again

"Teachers," said Leonard -
"Are my lessons done?"
"Did my singing please you?"
"Were the songs I sang so wrong?"

Leonard, it wasn't wrong it was a tower of song

Another tribute to Leonard

I stepped into an avalanche
It covered up my soul
I drew aside the curtains
And mocked the beauty if our world

The birds they sang
That wars they will be fought again
And that there's a crack in everything

cont.

That's how the light got in

I used to love the rainbow
I loved the early morning dew
But I cannot break the code
Of your frozen lies of truth

You know who I am
You've stared at the sun
And I cry O Lady Midnight
I feel that I grew old

I loved your body and your spirit
But I told you that I was not one of those
Yet still I want to walk with you a while
Across the sand and be your man

And now we are wounded
So deep and so well
But I cannot follow you my love and you cannot follow me

Dreaming

I dreamt of us together last night
We came out of the flat and it had been raining
We side-stepped the puddles
You had your warm coat on
I put my arms around your neck
We kissed each other
I turned to go
You said "you can't leave me now; I need you"
I woke up
"You left ME, remember?" I said
But you didn't answer
I watch romantic films
And remember how we were
I see Richard Geer and notice his hair's like yours
I watch a guy rubbing down a lady's back
To warm her after she was wet
Just like you did for me
I see people fall out and remember you saying

cont.

"What happened to us?"
I said "You kept taking Heroin"
Everyone watched us when we talked together
At work
I miss you
So much

Homage to Leonard Cohen

I was first aware of his beauty when I heard him
Singing Bird on a wire
He held the wings of desire
Did Leonard

I thought Dylan was good till I grew up
And heard Leonards Poems
Dylan couldn't even remember
Why he wrote some of his lyrics

Leonard spent days on every line he wrote
Spent a year on every song he sang
"A thousand kisses deep
Back on Boogie Street," "I'm your man"

He was full of gentleness and humility
Learnt from his time in the monastery
With the Zen Buddhist Roshi
Leonard became his friend and was ordained

"I know in your smile
That tonight will be fine
For a while"
My Commitment is writing poetry, he said

In his book Beautiful Losers
Leonard wrote in the Preface "Dear reader
Please forgive me if I have wasted your time
If you don't like them skip over the lines"

cont.

He read The Baghavad Gita where Krishna says
"You're a warrior of my choosing
This is just a play, arise my noble warrior
Embrace your destiny and do your duty"

I loved you baby way back then
And I will remember you well to this day
Sing Hallelujah in heaven
When you reawaken, noble warrior

Wales

After the funeral
"Come and stay with us
Think about it" she said
So I went to Crickhowell

Told her
I feel like a big stone is where my heart used to be
I'm sorry I've been so unhappy
I cried, but thank you for having me

Was dined and spoilt
And met her grand-daughter Elsie
And returned home
To my memories of Alan

They moved to Cyncoed
Was invited again after my grand-daughters wedding
Happier this time
And wined and dined again

Went to a waterfall
That wasn't falling anymore
Me and Georgie had time together
Talking of the past

Recovering past recollections
And reflections
Missed a train connection   cont.
Sign of the times

Home again naturally
Thank you both
For helping me in my time of need
It's been two years now and I'm okay

You're still my little sister
I used to read Hiawatha to
Thank you for being you

Picasso Man of Many Talents

Born in Malaga in Spain
Picasso took his mothers name
It was the birth of an Art revolution and his fame

"In art you have to kill your father"
Said Picasso
His fathers name was too long to handle

Picasso was an artist and a painter
A Ceramicist and a sculptor, a playwright
And a set designer - and a poet

"The incandescent crystal
That sings on the wing of the bees wax"
He penned in lyrics - and

"Its thousand lit candles
The green flocks of wool illuminated
By the gentle acrobatics of the lanterns"

Picasso's Art illuminated his feelings like a diary;
The Blue Period with sadness in his canvas
The Rose Period with serenity and Ecstasy

Paintings that showed fascination with society
"The OLD GUITARIST" and the "GUGGENHEIM"
Paintings about their struggle   cont.

With Poverty

Influenced by Cezanne they founded Cubism and
With Apollinaire and Breton became Surrealists
And his painting of "GUITARE" reveals its Idealism

In The Spanish Civil War Picasso felt the horror
And condemned the Fascist Nazis brutality
Resulting in his masterpiece of "GUERNICA"

Picasso's "DOVE OF PEACE" - another masterpiece
Chosen as a representative of The Peace
For the international Peace Conference in 1949
The police accused him of stealing
Da Vinci's painting of THE MONA LISA
Missing until found stolen by a security guard

Picasso inspired McCartney song "DRINK TO ME"
Picasso's last words being "Drink to my health
You know I can't drink anymore

A fitting end to an artist of many talents
Who now rests in heaven
And paints angels at his leisure

Corinne

"Will you do one for me?"
You said
So yer tis
My friend

You're a brilliant hairdresser
And friend
You gave me the number
For a clairvoyant one day
When I needed one, and she was good
Yvette was her name

Nicest thing you did for me
Was to give me a free hair do

cont.

To go to Alan's funeral
It looked amazing, everyone said so
Sometimes you put gold highlights in it
Sometimes you put copper streaks in it

You also gave me for Christmas
An inspirational word search book
Because you know I like word searches
While I'm waiting for my hair to be done
With sayings on every page - like
"How lovely yellow is! It stands for the sun"
Vincent Van Gough
You're amazing,
And you're a bit of a clairvoyant yourself

Sandra

An acquisition
Of a position in The Council
Was our introduction to each other
All those years ago
And we've been friends ever since

In the intricate way of the world
Our lives although separate
Ultimately followed similar lines
In our relationships

Neither of us criticised each other
In our decisions
Only commiserated
Over our experiences

We were going to travel
Down Route 66
Remember? A nice idea
Never came to fruition
Cos I never learnt to drive, that's why

cont.

You travelled to Canada and Spain
With Steve
I travelled to Morocco and America
With Alan
You gave me some precious gifts;

My book of the I-Ching
And my glass Buddha
And best of all
The precious gift of friendship
Which has lasted all these years

You're amazing

Nikki

She'd been waiting five years
For the operation
"Is it true? She asked the doctor
Did it really happen
or was I only dreaming?"

Yes my dear he said
I'm sorry it took so long
But the NHS
Are stretched
This time of year

We did well don't you know
And so did you, young lady
You should be proud of yourself
That you stuck to the diet
When we told you to

You were a model patient
Now go home and rest it
To your kids but they'll have to help you
In case you take a turn for the worse
Ask the nurse
Or we'll have to reverse
The operation

A Tuesday in November

Joe phoned, surprised but hesitant
Keith Phoned, for conversation
Dave phoned, for friendship
Phaedra phoned, for comfort
Taro played some music
Not such bad day -
Since I threw a book across the room

We Travelled the World

Riding camels
In Morocco and Spain
Rode an elephant
in Sri Lanka

Canoed down a river
In France
Climbed mountains
Etna in Sicily and Vesuvius in Italy

Saw dolphins leaping
In Spain
Caught a train
To Rome

Went on a steam train
In Wales
Hung upside down
On the Blarney Stone
In Ireland

Held snakes
In Marrakesh
Went on a cable car
In Portugal

Went on 'The Yellow Submarine'
In The Gran Canaries

cont.

Visited a Viking castle
In Denmark

Marvelled at Sunsets
Got caught in the rain
Camped up a mountain
And came home again

Clive

Sorry you died
Clive
Thanks for the eleven years
I'll forget about the tears
Thanks for the time you spent
With your son
Before you had to go
So soon
You played music together
On the moors
With keyboards and guitars
Musical Artists
You were both Stars
In my eyes

Phaedra and Taro
Full of heartbreak
Were so sad
When they heard the news
My heart ached for them
And for me too
Thanks for the memories
I had with you

I'll remember you
With Phaedra your baby
On the bed with you
And Taro your son
With you
On the moors

Going Back To The 60s

I was listening to Thy Byrds
Playing "Hey Mr Tambourine Man"
Cos Dylan was a friend of theirs
I was older than that then
I'm younger than that now
Just relax and pay it attention

Hey Mr Spaceman
Won't you please take me along
for the ride

There is a time
To every Season
Turn, Turn, Turn
A time to laugh
a time to weep
A time for Peace
(Makes me wonder)

And the summertime
Is coming
Will you go lassie go?

Across the purple Heather
Or down in my easy chair
I 'm not going anywhere

Or go back to the sixties
When we gave Peace a chance
And all that romance

Singing songs of Love and Peace
And handing out flowers
Will you go
Lassie
Go??

Under The Mulberry Tree

I walk in the garden
In the early morning dew
To hear the seagulls
High up in the sky
Crying for their mates
And laughing at me
The blackbird sits on the wall
Waiting for his mate
While the turtle dove
Keeps his beady eye on the garden
And the little sparrows twitter in the hedge
And the magpies gather their family together

It's been a good year for the roses
Three of them, sending their scents
All over the garden, red pink and white
And for the purple peonies in the maze
With the fuchsias
Hanging their lanterns

The Lonicera gold flame
Of honeysuckle grow up the trellises
With the purple violet Campanule
Growing in the wall
And giant forget-me-nots
Stand proud' waiting for the bees

But it's the Mulberry Tree
Which adds its splendour
To the scene
I wish you were here with me
Under the tree
Or smelling the roses
With me

Memories

Mount Edgecumbe and us in The Folly
Us in Mexico in the plush hotel
And riding in The Tram in San Francisco
Golden Gate Park and us playing frisbee
On the beach by the Golden Gate Bridge
Golden Gate Park reading the newspaper
"Protest Bush's Inauguration"
Your big smile in Corfu
With us and the quod bikes
The hammock Cafe
With you playing chess
Us on the elephant in Sri Lanka
With snakes around our necks
Eating ice-creams in the sunset
In Marrakesh outside 'The Souk'
In the Atlas Mountains
Dressed as Arabs with the camels
Holding the baby Argan goats
In Essaouira with tea and cakes
You in Italy with The Times newspaper
Me in Pompeii with the white hat
You in the back streets of Naples
In Taormina in the ruins eating Gnocchi
Us on Mount Etna on top of the world
In France canoeing down the river
In Cyprus in the run-down shack
Riding Horses and camels in Spain
In The Yellow Submarine
You with the giant Buddha
In a cable-car in Portugal
Up in the mountains and on the tram in Porto
In The Holiday Inn in Belgium
Outside the Hindu Temple in Sri Lanka
Having a beer on the beach in Colombo
Us in Amsterdam
Riding the waves in Spain
With the dolphins playing games
In The Honeymoon suite in Pompeii
Memories are made of this

The Mermaid's Lament

I'll tell you of a mermaid fair
Who sings upon a rock
And every time she sheds a tear
She fills the sea with salt

She plays upon a golden harp
Sweet music fills the air
And when she tires of singing songs
She combs her golden hair

Fair mermaid sings the saddest song
Her voice is like a lark
Her song which is about her love
A love which broke her heart

My lover was a handsome prince
Who lived upon the land
But as I lived in waters deep
He could not take my hand

He came to see me every day
We sat upon this rock
He asked me if I'd be his bride
I said alas that I cannot

"I could not live upon the sand
The ocean is my life
I could not walk upon the shore
I cannot be your wife"

My Prince he took me in his arms
He kissed my tears away
He sadly looked into my eyes
"Sweet mermaid fare thee well"

"Since that day, I have not seen
My handsome Prince again"
And so, she sings upon the rock
The mermaid's sad lament.

Mary's other books

This is not the first time Mary has published her work. In 2016 Mary published a travel diary together with Alan Burnett called 'AFTER THE RAIN a journey around Europe by campervan' which documented their travels from The Netherlands to France, Germany, Denmark, Poland, The Czech Republic and Switzerland leaving the reader with useful tips of places to stay and interesting facts about different countries, encouraging others to leave the comfort of their armchairs to visit and explore different countries and meet diverse people around Europe. Alan and Mary took it in turns to give their own daily comments on the experiences they went through together which are both amusing and honest and gives their travels a welcome break from just being a factual account of driving in Betty, their campervan.

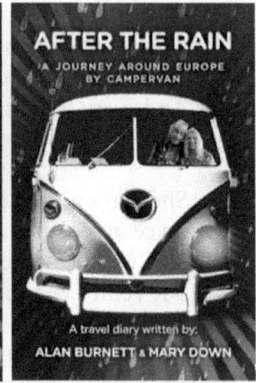

Mary also has her work published in the Penny Authors' Book of lived volume 10" (2024)

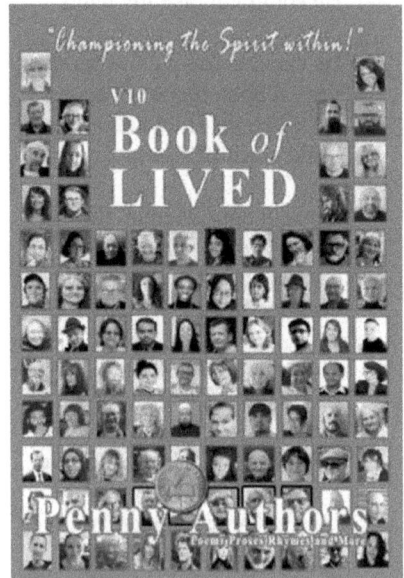

More information about Penny Authors is available from the website: www.pennyauthors.org.uk.

All publishing and book catalogue information can be found on the website
www.mapublisher.org.uk

www.ingramcontent.com/pod-product-compliance
Lightning Source LLC
Chambersburg PA
CBHW071102090426
42737CB00013B/2430